Winter 1982 Volume V Number 4

Paperback Quarterly

*"Journal of
Mass-Market Paperback History"*

Contents

The Career of David Goodis
   by Geoffrey O'Brien..3

T.H.R.U.S.H.'s Insidious Weapons or
"What Will They Think of Next?"
   by Bruce Barnes...13

The Paperback Hall of Fame of Miscellaneous
Curiosities, Part III: Cover Art Sharing
   by Daniel G. Roberts...19

Isador N. Steinberg: Profile of an Artist
   by Piet Schreuders..29

Science-Fiction and Fantasy in the Dell Mapbacks
   by W. H. Lyles..40

Nelson Algren in Paperback: A Checklist
   by Paul Garon...50

Covers That Never Were
   by Piet Schreuders..61

WILDSIDE PRESS

Paperback Quarterly specializes in the history of mass market paperbacks

Paperback Quarterly features articles and notes dealing with every type (mystery, detective, science fiction, western, adventure, etc) and with every aspect of new, old and rare paperbacks.

Emphasis is placed on the historical research of paperbacks, their authors, illustrators, publishers and distributors, but the editors also invite contributions of bibliographical interest. In short, the only criterion for the editors' consideration is that the subject matter pertain to paperbacks.

Paperback Quarterly pays 2¢ per word (200-2000 words) for articles and notes. Payment also includes two copies of the issue in which your article appears.

Paperback Quarterly is published in Spring, Summer, Fall and Winter of each year with a subscription rate of $12.00 per year or individual copies for $3.95 each. Institutional and library subscriptions are $15.00 per year. Overseas rate is $15.00. All back issues are out of print.

All correspondence, articles, notes, queries, ads and subscriptions should be sent to 1710 Vincent, Brownwood, Texas 76801. (915) 643-1182.

Ad rate card on request.

Published and Edited by

Charlotte Laughlin   Billy C. Lee

Contributing Editors

Bill Crider   Michael S. Barson
William Lyles   Thomas L. Bonn
Piet Schreuders

Printer and Technical Advisor
Martin E. Gottschalk

Copy Editor
Judy Crider

Cover logo designed by Peter Manesis

Copyright © 1982 by Billy C. Lee
All Rights Reserved
Printed in the United States of America

The Career of David Goodis
by Geoffrey O'Brien

David Goodis (1917-1967) was one of the most distinctive stylists among writers of paperback originals; at the very least it can be said that a page of his work is instantly recognizable. A native of Philadelphia, which provided the background for most of his books, he graduated from Temple University in 1938, the same year his first novel (RETREAT FROM OBLIVION) was published. The book apparently did not fare too well with the critics. A reviewer in BOOKS remarked: "The opening sentence of RETREAT FROM OBLIVION is as follows: 'After a while it gets so bad that you want to stop the whole business.' It refers to Herb's state of mind, but it's not an inaccurate summary of what one is inclined to say about David Goodis' novel" In any event, for the next decade he shifted over to the pulps. If "Red Wings for the Doomed" (an aviation novella published in the January 1941 issue of BATTLE BIRDS) is indicative, his pulp writing had little individuality; however, the experience undoubtedly developed the narrative craft which keeps his novels from dissolving into a morass of psychological analysis. Later he went to Hollywood, working in turn for Universal and Warner Brothers; his only significant credit was as co-writer on THE UNFAITHFUL, Vincent Sherman's 1947 remake of THE LETTER.

In 1947 Goodis' second novel, DARK PASSAGE, made considerably more of a splash than his first. The jazzlike flow of the prose earned him some attention as a stylist, and the intricate, nowadays not too believable plot (one of the first new-face-through-plastic-surgery stories) became the basis for a Bogart-Bacall vehicle. This was followed by BEHOLD THIS WOMAN, a dismal

Geoffrey O'Brien is the author of *Hardboiled America: The Lurid Years of Paperbacks.*

exercise in the LEAVE HER TO HEAVEN wicked woman genre. The book is fascinating as a glimpse of Goodis' erotic obsessions, but cannot have done much for his reputation as a writer. The next one, however, was his most balanced and perhaps most appealing novel: NIGHTFALL (later issued by Lion as THE DARK CHASE). Here he eschewed the trickiness of DARK PASSAGE and constructed a simple but compelling narrative of an innocent man on the run recounted in his tightest prose. Goodis creates an atmosphere in which everything is symbolic -- the oppressive heat of a summer night, a metal box of water colors that crashes to the floor, the winding stairs on which the hero flees -- and at the same time densely literal.

An undistinguished police procedural story (OF MISSING PERSONS) was to be Goodis' farewell to cloth covers. (It might be noted that when Goodis identifies himself with the police, his inspiration dries up, but when he writes of criminals his prose soars.) The move to paperback originals ushers in a radical change in the style and content of his work. As if mirroring the failure of Goodis' higher-toned literary ambitions, the novels turn decisively toward the lower depths. From here on he will be the chronicle of skid row, and more often than not of the man fallen from his social class, the disgraced airline pilot (CASSIDY'S GIRL), the artist turned art appraiser for a gang of burglars (BLACK FRIDAY), the famous crooner turned street corner bum (STREET OF NO RETURN), the concert performer transformed into barroom piano player (DOWN THERE). Thus Goodis transmutes his own vision of himself as great literary artist transformed into paperback hack writer.

CASSIDY'S GIRL (1951), the first of his nine Gold Medal novels, was evidently the most popular, judging from the number of times Fawcett

Lion #LB131 Lion #186

Pocket Book #833 Books by David Goodis Bantam #407

reprinted it. (It was again reissued by Dell in 1967, the year of Goodis' death.) It contains most of the elements of the later novels: an environment of grinding poverty, a sensitive but inarticulate male protagonist apparently unaware of his self-destructive tendencies, and two women who divide his energy, with melodramatic consequences: one a frail, ghostly alcoholic haunted by ethereal dreams (let us call her Type A), the other a fat, rough-tongued, hard-drinking (and hard-fighting) woman who will stop at nothing to keep the hero to herself (Type B). There are many recurring relationships in Goodis' novels, but this polarity between two images of woman is always central; and the hero, caught up by his own lack of self-knowledge, is usually destroyed by it. He sees Type A as his true love, his only hope for happiness, from whom he is kept apart by Type B, to whom he is bound either by marriage, by blackmail, or even by the threat of physical force. What he can never admit is that he himself in some way sets up the no-win situation, and that indeed it is the Type B woman, that obese and muscular caricature of female dominance, that he really desires.

STREET OF THE LOST (1952) is the most ham-handed of the Gold Medal books, emphasizing the prolonged fistfights which were a Goodis sideline -- he evidently had at least a fan's knowledge of boxing, and so his accounts have a somewhat pedantic precision -- and the even more prolonged drinking bouts which began to dominate his fiction (and, one surmises, his life). The following book, OF TENDER SIN (1952), is a sort of poor man's LOST WEEKEND, in which Al Darby (one of Goodis' occasional white-collar heroes), tormented by the impotence which is destroying his marriage, embarks on an epic binge, revisiting the impoverished scenes of his youth, playing out a paranoid fantasy almost to the point of committing murder, receiving wisdom from an old Negro on skid row (one of many philosophical bums to follow), and ultimately summoning up the repressed memory of an incestuous episode which is supposed to be the root of his troubles. Many of Goodis' novels follow a similar psychoanalytic pattern; the thrust of his books is always toward release, redemption, resolution of conflict, and there are even some theoretically "happy" endings; but whatever salvation Goodis as author may cook up for his characters, it is clearly nothing but literary wishful thinking. The despair does not go away.

THE BURGLAR (1953) was the first of three books that Goodis wrote for Lion. These were sharper-edged than the Gold Medal novels, suggesting an editorial hand excising some of the author's more uncontrolled descents into self-pity. THE BURGLAR (which was later filmed by Paul Wendkos, with a screenplay by Goodis himself, and co-starring the oddly paired Dan Duryea and Jayne Mansfield) is notable for its curious prose style, which in spots reads like a pulp version of Jack Kerouac before the fact; perhaps Kerouac read THE BURGLAR somewhere along the road. In its back cover blurb Lion proclaimed: "Twenty years ago it was HAMMETT...for the first time telling the crime story with raw and savage truth...Ten years ago it was CHANDLER... taking the realism one step further—into the nightmare world of a murderer's mind...Today it is DAVID GOODIS...pushing the crime novel forward into a new dimension—probing into the heart of the thief and the killer." Whatever the accuracy of this as literary history, it pinpoints Goodis' originality quite well. The strength of his novels is the way in which his characters' emotions color every sentence, every bit of physical description. At his best Goodis endows his icy streets and wretched shanties with an expressionistic intensity; at his worst he merely overwrites, providing in the process a devastatingly accurate picture of an alcoholic mind in its own circular patterns.

The central law of Goodis' fiction is that happiness is forbidden. All true love remains unconsummated; all petty criminals (a breed with whom the author obviously identifies) are caught ignominiously; all proud old men are humiliated; all virgins are molested. The sentimental lyricism of Goodis' prose masks a savage perception of life. In THE MOON IN THE GUTTER (1953), a dockworker's sister is raped; she slits her throat with a razor in a garbage-strewn alleyway. Later in the book, a slumming socialite tyring to seduce the dockworker drives him over to the harbor, saying "It's really magnificent." He replies with a nauseating description of the smell and texture of bilgewater, and when she recoils adds: "I'm only trying to give you the full picture. You come down to see the dirt, I'm showing you the dirt." In a memorable final episode he indicts the moon shining above the gutter (hence the title) for his sister's death.

Of the three novels Goodis wrote in 1954, Gold Medal's STREET OF NO RETURN epitomizes his vision of skid row. Three bums stand on a corner trying to figure out how to get a drink; one of them wanders off and comes back 175 pages later, a bottle under his coat, having relived his entire life: his career as a pop singer shattered by an obsessive love for a prostitute, his torture by racketeers and his beating at the hands of the police, his final turn as a reluctant hero foiling a conspiracy to foment a race riot--only to find that all he really wants to do is to go back to the corner. Here Goodis came closest to acknowledging that his heroes' tragic destinies were largely self-created. His battered protagonist finally admits to himself: "You've played a losing game and actually enjoyed the idea of losing, almost like them freaks who get their kicks when they're banged around ..."

Gold Medal Paperback Originals by David Goodis

You're in that same bracket, buddy. You're one of them less-than-nothings who like the taste of being hurt." He moves inevitably toward the book's final sentence: "They sat there passing the bottle around, and there was nothing that could bother them, nothing at all." Similarly, the artist hero of BLACK FRIDAY, having witnessed the violent collapse of the gang of burglars he has joined and the self-sacrificing death of the pale girl he loves, walks off into the night: "He had no idea where he was going and he didn't care."

A key to all this inner turmoil can be found in THE BLONDE ON THE STREET CORNER, a period piece set in the 1930's which has all the earmarks of an autobiographical novel. The young hero, whose family struggles for survival on the lower fringes of the middle class, is an aspiring songwriter still buoyed by the optimism of youth. The novel is essentially the story of how his hopes are nipped in the bud as he yields to the aggressive advances of the blonde of the title, a violent, alcoholic older woman who brings him face to face with his real sexual nature. This stands alone in Goodis' work, and is by the way another example of Lion Books' remarkable openness to the offbeat.

THE WOUNDED AND THE SLAIN (1955) gives us another white-collar drunk, on vacation in Jamaica with his frigid wife and doing best to get himself killed in barroom brawls. This is Goodis' most thorough dissection of alcoholism, but the book rapidly loses credibility as the hero becomes accidentally involved with the Kingston underworld and ends by triumphing over his problems. Far more successful is DOWN THERE (1956), best known as the source of Francois Truffaut's SHOOT THE PIANO PLAYER. Here Goodis blends two of his favorite themes--the artist on the skids and the criminal gang as a surrogate family (in this case the gang is a family)--to produce one of his most satisfying novels.

His next book, FIRE IN THE FLESH (1957), is the unlikely tale of a pyromaniac who discovers that the only way he can control his impulses is by drinking cheap wine. In a final catharsis he discovers the roots of his obsession and is cured. NIGHT SQUAD (1961), a distinctly minor work, concerns a crooked cop turned alcoholic who likewise finds redemption at the eleventh hour. Goodis' last novel, the posthumously published SOMEBODY'S DONE FOR (1967), is a kind of pot-pourri of his major themes--the two women, the gang/family, alcoholism, impotence, incest--played out on a barren strip of New Jersey shoreline. These final books, apparently reflecting the author's state of mind, are suffused with a depression that creeps into the rhythm of the sentences.

From about midway in his career Goodis shows every sign of having reached an impasse in his personal life. The obsessions which are laid bare in his novles begin to repeat themselves rather than to develop creatively. But taken as a whole his work represents an astonishing example of self-revelation in the contex of genre fiction. It is interesting that he was able for so long to sustain a career in paperbacks; today the kind of low-keyed emotional realism he practiced, with its downbeat emphasis on personal and social failure, would find little response among publishers. In any case his novels remain fascinating both for the intensity and the vernacular eloquence of the writing and for the passion with which Goodis expresses the point of view of the lowest of social outcasts.

The author is indebted to Jhan Robbins and Knox Burger for sharing their recollections of Goodis, and to the Goodis bibliography which appeared in POLAR #10 (Paris, 1980).

Books by David Goodis

HARDCOVER:
  1938--RETREAT FROM OBLIVION (Dutton).
  1946--DARK PASSAGE (Messner; pb Dell#221 in 1948)
  1947--BEHOLD THIS WOMAN (Appleton Century;
      pb Bantam #407 in 1948 and Popular
      Library #775 in 1956)
  1947--NIGHTFALL (Messner; pb Lion Library #131
      in 1956)
  1950--OF MISSING PERSONS (Morrow; pb Pocket
      Books #833 in 1951)

PAPERBACK ORIGINALS:
  1951--CASSIDY'S GIRL (Gold Medal #189 in 1951
      and #544 in 1956; reprinted by Dell
      in 1967)
  1952--STREET OF THE LOST (Gold Medal #256 in
      1952 and #652 in 1957)
  1952--OF TENDER SIN (Gold Medal #226 in 1952
      and #626 in 1956)
  1953--THE BURGLAR (Lion #124)
  1953--THE MOON IN THE GUTTER (Gold Medal #348)
  1954--BLACK FRIDAY (Lion #224)
  1954--STREET OF NO RETURN (Gold Medal #428)
  1954--THE BLONDE ON THE STREET CORNER (Lion
      #186)
  1955--THE WOUNDED AND THE SLAIN (Gold Medal
      #530)
  1956--DOWN THERE (Gold Medal #623; reprinted
      by Black Cat as SHOOT THE PIANO PLAYER)
  1957--FIRE IN THE FLESH (Gold Medal #691)
  1961--NIGHT SQUAD (Gold Medal #s1083)
  1967--SOMEBODY'S DONE FOR (Banner)

Partially compiled with the help of Robert
Reginald's CUMULATIVE PAPERBACK INDEX, 1939-1959.

T.H.R.U.S.H.'s Insidious Weapons
or
"What Will They Think of Next?"
by Bruce Barnes

During the mid 1960's, with the Cold War as cold as ever, any story involving the allies in mortal combat against some evil and mysterious enemy was given a better than average chance of becomming a hit. The best examples of this genre are Ian Fleming's James Bond novels and subsequent films. Inspired by their success, an American television producer, Norman Felton, called on Fleming. According to Richard Meyers, Fleming was "responsive when Felton asked if he would create a superspy specifically for television. According to reports, Fleming simply recycled a minor Sicilian character from his DIAMONDS ARE FOREVER, and came up with Napoleon Solo." [1]

 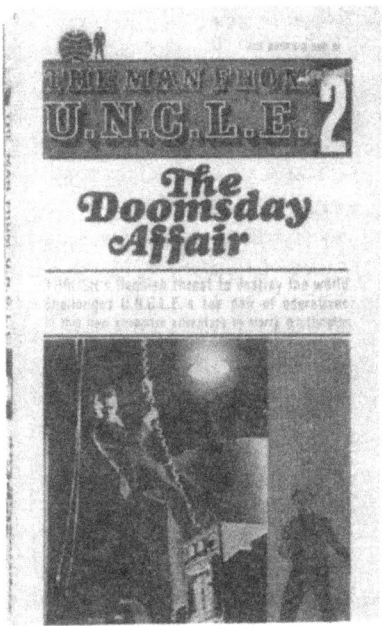

The Man From U.N.C.L.E. #1 and #2

Given its creator, it is hardly surprising that The Man from U.N.C.L.E. (the United Network Command for Law and Enforcement) became a very popular television program. Accompanying the TV effort was a series of twenty-one novels, published by Ace Books, and written by such authors as Michael Avallone and Harry Whittington.

Each of the novels deals with the exploits of U.N.C.L.E.'S top two agents, Napoleon Solo and Illya Kuryakin. Together, they battle the encroachment of T.H.R.U.S.H. (Technological Hierarchy for the Removal of Undesireables and Subjugation of Humanity). Essentially, The Man from U.N.C.L.E. presents the Cold War with a twist; reds in Hollywood or Congress have become passe, as have fears of an air raid at any hour of the day or night. Here, U.N.C.L.E. agents are up against some of the most diabolical weapons in the history of espionage. Summaries of the first five (and probably best) U.N.C.L.E. books follow.

The Man from U.N.C.L.E. no. 1; THE THOUSAND COFFINS AFFAIR by Michael Avallone, Ace G-553÷- In a bizarre state of affairs, the entire population of two small communities on opposite sides of the globe are striken with unexplainable symptoms: All the inhabitants begin to babble incoherently, and die in a matter of hours. The cadavers then undergo amazingly rapid decomposition. When a fellow agent dies of these same symptoms, Napoleon and Illya are assigned to investigate. They learn that T.H.R.U.S.H. is behind this small scale holocaust; by means of a small pellet, the chemicals that cause the fatal symptoms are introduced into the bloodstream of the desired victim. Millions of these pellets are buried in coffins in Orangeberg Cemetary, located outside a small German town of the same name. Since the other U.N.C.L.E. agent was killed in Orangeberg, Napoleon and Illya have little trouble in discovering and destroying all the coffins, and the pellets along with them.

The Man from U.N.C.L.E. no. 2; THE DOOMSDAY AFFAIR by Harry Whittington, Ace G-560--A ruthless man, Tixe Ylno ("Exit Only" spelled backwards) has, by bribes or by blackmail, persuaded the world's most prominent scientists to design an atomic device for him. Mr. Ylno turns out to be a former Presidential advisor who has lost his security clearance. He plans to bomb the world's major powers and declare himself ruler of the world, once the remains have stopped smouldering. With T.H.R.U.S.H. as his ally, he poses a significant threat. U.N.C.L.E. comes to the rescue, however, just in time to save the world from rule by a White House reject, and the international Status Quo remains intact.

The Man from U.N.C.L.E. no. 3; THE COPENHAGEN AFFAIR by John Oram, Ace G-564--T.H.R.U.S.H. has developed a startling new weapon in its plan for world conquest. Put simply, this new device is a flying saucer with an H-bomb inside. Agent Garbridge, who operates T.H.R.U.S.H.'s Swedish and Danish satraps, is supervising the research on the saucers, which are manufactured in an underground factory in Denmark. Aided by Danish U.N.C.L.E. agents, our two heroes infiltrate the factory and detonate the H-bombs. Due to the underground location of the factory, there is no danger of fallout. The T.H.R.U.S.H. agents in charge of the factory die in an attempt to escape.

The Man from U.N.C.L.E. no. 4; THE DAGGER AFFAIR by David McDaniel, Ace G-571--In a rare turn of events, U.N.C.L.E. and T.H.R.U.S.H. combine forces to combat another organization, Dagger (which, refreshingly, is not an acronym or anagram for <u>anything</u>). The head of Dagger is Kim Keldur, a young Nihilist who, convinced of the evil and corrupt nature of mankind, is bent on the destruction of the human race. Furthermore, he has invented a machine called the Energy Damper, which is designed to carry out his plan. Both T.H.R.U.S.H. and U.N.C.L.E. realize that their respective plans for the world are in jeopardy, and after an interesting series of cloak and dagger hijinks, they corner Keldur. In a do or die effort, he activates the Damper, creating a rapidly spreading field that kills all energy within it. T.H.R.U.S.H. has prepared for just such a possibility, however, and crashes a remote-controlled airplane into Keldur's device. The kinetic energy of the plane conteracts that of the damper, and Keldur dies in the insuing explosion. Having accomplished their joint mission, U.N.C.L.E. and T.H.R.U.S.H. end their unlikely alliance.

The Man from U.N.C.L.E. no. 5, THE MAD SCIENTIST AFFAIR by John Phillifent, Ace G-581-- Michael O'Rourke, an Irish biochemist, has constructed a molecule that will, in his own words, "have the world at my mercy." The molecule, which O'Rourke has concealed in cans of

The Man From U.N.C.L.E. #3 and #4

beer, takes away all cautionary impulses from the person who ingests it. The possibilities for college campuses alone are terrifying, but when one considers that O'Rourke and T.H.R.U.S.H. (his newly found friend) plan to use it on the world's armies, the danger becomes clear. Having been assigned to stop the beer and O'Rourke, Napoleon and Illya enlist the help of O'Rourke's niece. They gain entrance to the brewery and explode all the affected cans, thus enabling the world to crack open a cool one in relative safety.

1. Richard Meyers, TV DETECTIVES, San Diego. A. S. Barnes & Company, Inc. 1981, p 96.

List of U.N.C.L.E. Books

#1 THE THOUSAND COFFINS by Michael Avallone, Ace G-553*and Ace 51669. 50¢
#2 THE DOOMSDAY AFFAIR by Harry Whittington, Ace G-560* and Ace 51671. 50¢
#3 THE COPENHAGEN AFFAIR by John Oram, Ace G-564* and Ace 51673. 50¢
#4 THE DAGGER AFFAIR by David McDaniel, Ace G-571* and Ace 51675. 50¢
#5 THE MAD SCIENTIST AFFAIR by John T. Phillifent, Ace G-581* and 51677. 50¢
#6 THE VAMPIRE AFFAIR by David McDaniel, Ace 51679. 50¢
#7 THE RADIOACTIVE CAMEL AFFAIR by Peter Leslie, Ace 51681. 50¢
#8 THE MONSTER WHEEL AFFAIR by David McDaniel, Ace 51683. 50¢
#9 THE DIVING DAMES AFFAIR by Peter Leslie, Ace 51685. 50¢
#10 THE ASSASSINATION AFFAIR by J. Hunter Holly, Ace 51687. 50¢
#11 THE INVISIBILITY AFFAIR by Thomas Stratton, Ace 51689. 50¢

#12 THE MIND TWISTERS AFFAIR by Thomas Stratton, Ace 51691. 50¢
#13 THE RAINBOW AFFAIR by David McDaniel, Ace 51693. 50¢
#14 THE CROSS OF GOLD AFFAIR by Fredric Davies, Ace 51695. 50¢
#15 THE UTOPIA AFFAIR by David McDaniel, Ace 51697. 50¢
#16 THE SPLINTERED SUNGLASSES AFFAIR by Peter Leslie, Ace 51699. 50¢
#17 THE HOLLOW CROWN AFFAIR by David McDaniel, Ace 51700. 50¢
#18 THE UNFAIR FARE AFFAIR by Peter Leslie, Ace 51701. 50¢
#19 THE POWER CUBE AFFAIR by John T. Phillifent, Ace 51702. 50¢
#20 THE CORFU AFFAIR by John T. Phillifent, Ace 51703. 50¢
#21 THE THINKING MACHINE AFFAIR by Joel Bernard, Ace 51704. 50¢

 * The first five books (and probably more) were assigned a "G" book number. They were later all given a ISBN identification.

25¢
OLD PAPERBACKS
(DIGESTS, PULPS)
BOUGHT-SOLD
TOM NIGRA
(201) 634-7105

865 DIANE COURT WOODBRIDGE, N.J. 07095

The Paperback Hall of Fame of Miscellaneous Curiosities, Part III: Cover Art Sharing
by Daniel G. Roberts

Presented herein is the last in a three-part series describing a number of curiosities appearing in Paperback Quarterly Volume 5, No.'s 2 and 3, highlighted examples of errata and cover and printing variations. This installment is concerned entirely with examples of shared cover art.

As conceptualized here, cover art sharing includes any examples of the same cover illustration appearing on one or more paperback books, normally with entirely different titles and, frequently, content. While not occurring with the frequency that errata or cover/printing variations seem to, shared cover art nevertheless does occur with some regularity, with some publishing houses, in particular Avon, engaging in the practice more than others. Those examples listed below, in fact, may only be the tip of the iceberg.

COVER ART SHARING

1) Bantam 146: Philip MacDonald, THE RYNOX MURDER MYSTERY
    Bantam 148: Robert George Dean, ON ICE
    Bantam 150: Liam O'Falherty, THE INFORMER
    Bantam 151: Frank Gruber, THE NAVY COLT

In 1948, Bantam re-released a number of Superior Reprint titles, each with new Bantam dustjackets. The four titles noted above were all issued with the same cover illustration adorning their dustjackets, in which a frightened woman is framed by a pair of hands (doubtless belonging to a criminal, as

suggested by excessively bristly hair upon
the knuckles) loading a revolver. While each
cover illustration is rendered primarily in
yellow, there are subtle differences in the
white shading treatments surrounding the
hands. In the Dean title, the edges of the
shading are smooth, nearly paralleling the
shape of the hands exactly. In the O'Flaherty
and Gruber titles, however, the shading can
be described as "sunburst" style one each,
except that on the latter it is much more
jagged and pronounced. Finally, the
MacDonald title exhibits no shading whatso-
ever; instead, the white shading has been
extended to the cover margins, at the total
expense of the yellow rendering which
appears on each of the other three titles.
Rumor has it that Bantam 149 (Harrison R.
Steeves' GOODNIGHT SHERIFF) also has a
variation of the same dustjacket. Can this
be substantiated?

2) Avon 104: William Irish, IF I SHOULD DIE
BEFORE I WAKE, and Avon Murder Mystery
Monthly 13: Kelley Roos, IF THE SHROUD FITS

Both of these Avon mystery titles from the
mid-1940's bear the same front cover illustration, which depicts a wary young girl
eyeing a coffin and a human hand brandishing
a dagger. Except for the logo and title
design, the cover art is precisely identical.

3) Pyramid N3557: Maxwell Grant, HANDS IN THE
DARK (Shadow No. 4);
Pyramid N3699: Maxwell Grant, THE CRIME
CULT (Shadow No. 6), 1st & 2nd prints

Another example of "cheating" by using the
same cover illustration on different books
is provided by the recent reprinting of

selected Shadow novels by Pyramid. The first printing (January, 1975) of Shadow No. 4 has a Jim Steranko cover illustration depicting Lamont Cranston blazing away with his automatic from behind a gold sarcophagus, while the first printing (March 1975) of Shadow No. 6 shows the Shadow framed by a bloody hand clutching a crumpled piece of paper. Nothing unusual here but, for an as yet inexplicable reason, when Pyramid issued a second printing (November 1976) of Shadow No. 6, they used the sarcophagus illustration originally adorning No. 4. Was this by design or by mistake?

4) Avon 78: Noel Coward, TO STEP ASIDE
   Avon 105: Donald Henderson Clarke, LADY ANN

   Another example of Avon's use of identical, or nearly identical, front cover illustrations on different books occurs with these two titles issued in 1946. Both have the same cover illustration featuring a seemingly chagrined gentleman and a smugly confident woman. On the Coward title, however, the background is a shadowy brown, while on the Clarke title it is pure white. Otherwise, the illustrations are identical.

5) Berkley X1735: R. T. M. Scott, THE SPIDER STRIKES (Spider No. 1)
   Berkley (no number): R. T. M. Scott, THE WHEEL OF DEATH (Spider No. 2)

   When Berkley began its ill-fated venture in 1969 of publishing reprints of the pulp stories featuring the Spider, they hit upon two gimmicks to try to promote sales. The first was to issue THE WHEEL OF DEATH as a "Free Bonus Book with Purchase of Spider No. 1." This book, obviously, was issued with no cover price, nor did it have an identifying number. The second gimmick was to include the first page of the succeeding Spider novel as the last page in the previous issue. Accordingly, Spider No. 1 ends with a tantalizing look at the first page of Spider No. 2, notwithstanding, of course, the fact that both were obtained in their entirety for the price of one! In addition, Berkley, like Avon, utilized the same cover illustrations on more than one book, since the back cover illustration of Spider No. 1 appears in identical renditions on both the front and back covers of the free bonus book. Oh well, we shouldn't expect frills on a freebie!

6) Phantom 507 and Harlequin 168: Day Keene, HUNT THE KILLER

These two books of the same title by Day Keene both feature the same cover art, in which an embracing couple is threatened by a club-wielding thug. The Harlequin title, however, is rendered in harsh brownish-red tones, while the Phantom rendition appears in subdued bluish-purple. Interestingly, both editions advertise that each is an original and not a reprint. Since the Phantom edition indicates a release in 1951, while the Harlequin indicates a 1952 printing, it appears Harlequin was engaging in deceptive advertising.

7) Avon 272: Robert Briffault, EUROPA
   Avon T-115: A. Meritt, SEVEN FOOTPRINTS TO SATAN

One of the most interesting examples of cover art sharing is exemplified by the two titles noted above. On first glance, the classic

The Crime Cult
see curiosity #3

The Wheel of Death
see curiosity #5

Front cover of *Fingerman* (left) and back cover of *Song Without Sermon* (right)--see curiosity #8b

bondage cover appearing on Avon 272 (discussed as well in the previous installment on Cover/Printing Variations--see PAPERBACK QUARTERLY Volume 5, No. 3) seems to have been faithfully reproduced on Avon T-115. The same naked and bound damsel and menacing thug appear on both covers. Upon closer inspection, however, it can readily be seen that the rendition appearing on the later Merritt title has been considerably "softened" as compared to that appearing on the earlier Briffault title. While the Briffault title shows the thug wielding a bull-whip, which presumably is responsible for the two criss-crossing scars apparent on the damsel's back, the Merritt title shows no scars, while the thug, rather than brandishing a bull-whip, instead wields a length of rope, possibly a hangman's noose. Although the titles are entirely different, this "softening" is wholly reminiscent of a similar treatment applied to the second printing of Dell 542 (discussed in PAPERBACK QUARTERLY Volume 5, No. 3) and doubtless was precipitated by public or governmental outcry or investigation.

8) 1950's Front and Back Cover Art Sharing at Avon

In the early 1950's, Avon apparently economized in its cover art, utilizing numerous illustrations previously adorning front covers on the back covers of later, differently titled, books. In most cases, the back cover illustrations appeared on black and white or color-overdubbed renditions of the original artwork, and normally were cropped considerably from the original. In some cases, the original images were reversed in mirror fashion on the back covers. In at least one case (Avon 504, see below) the back cover illustration was not an actual reproduction, but rather a newly drawn imitation of the original, causing one to wonder why a totally new illustration was not commissioned The following Avon books, at the least, have shared front and back cover illustrations. Others doubtlessly exist.

a) No. 211: Robert Bloch, THE SCARF OF PASSION (front cover)
   No. 534: Robert Paul Smith, TIME AND THE PLACE (back cover)

b) No. 219: Raymond Chandler, FINGERMAN (front cover)
   No. 304: James Woolf, SONG WITHOUT SERMON (back cover)

c) No. 260: James T. Farrell, YESTERDAY'S LOVE (front cover)
   No. 381: James Hilton, NOTHING SO STRANGE (back cover)

d) No. 263: Herbert Asbury, THE GANGS OF NEW YORK (front cover)
   No. 384: Donald Henderson Clarke, LOUIS BERETTI (back cover)

e) No. 274: Lawrence Treat, T AS IN TRAPPED (front cover)
   No. 326: David Dortort, BURIAL OF THE FRUIT (back cover)
   No. 504: Richard G. Hubler, THE CHASE (back cover, imitation)

f) No. 292: Willard Weiner, FOUR BOYS, A GIRL, AND A GUN (front cover)
   No. 372: Irving Shulman, CRY TOUGH! (back cover)

Front cover of *The Gangs of New York* (left) and back cover of *Louis Beretti* (right)--see curiosity #8d

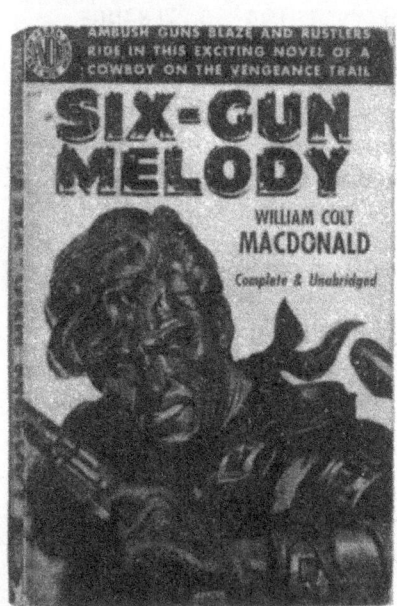
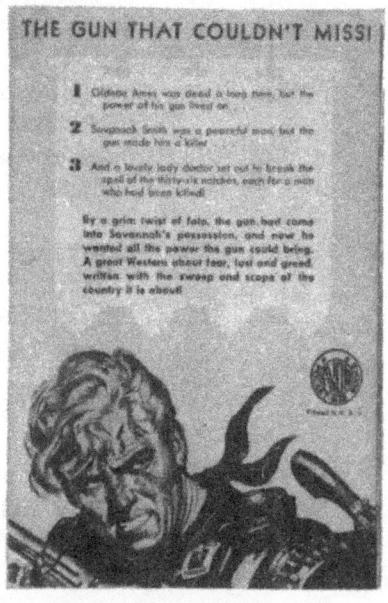

Front cover of *Six-Gun Melody* (left) and back cover of *The Marshall of Deer Creek* (right)--see curiosity #8j

g) No. 298: Felice Swados, HOUSE OF FURY (front cover)
No. 328: Dorothy L. Sayers, STRONG POISON (back cover)

h) No. 303: Robert Sylvester, DREAM STREET (front cover)
No. 390: Philip Wylie, THE SAVAGE GENTLEMAN (back cover)

i) No. 321: Leslie Charteris, THE SAINT IN NEW YORK (front cover)
No. 440: Leslie Charteris, SAINT AT THE THIEVE'S PICNIC (front cover)

j) No. 343: William Colt MacDonald, SIX-GUN MELODY (front cover)
No. 378: Al Cody, THE MARSHALL OF DEER CREEK (back cover)

k) No. 344: Earl Derr Biggers, THE CHINESE PARROT (front cover)
No. 393: Marc Brandel, THE MORON (back cover)

l) No. 314: Carl Van Vechten, NIGGER HEAVEN (front cover)
No. 400: George Wylie Henderson, JULE, ALABAMA BOY IN HARLEM (back cover)

m) No. 66: W. R. Burnett, LITTLE CEASAR (front cover)
No. 329: W. R. Burnett, LITTLE CEASAR (back cover)

n) Nos 185 & 419: Nelson Algren, NEVER COME MORNING (front covers)
No. 402: Jack Woodward, DANGEROUS LOVE (back cover)

o) No. 315: A. Merritt, THE METAL MONSTER (front cover)

No. 370:   A. Merritt, THE MOON POOL (back cover)

p)No. 301: James Hilton, WE ARE NOT ALONE (front cover)
No. 408:   Donald Henderson Clarke, TAWNY (back cover)

    With this installment, the three-part series on paperback curiosities comes to a close. It should again be noted, indeed emphasized, that the examples presented in each of the three installments are by no means thought to be exhaustive. Since most reside in my own collection, however, (with the remainder being brought to my attention by reliable sources) all can positively be substantiated. It should further be noted that, since my collection does not include many digests nor any comic books, the former may have been unduly slighted in the foregoing presentations, while the latter category was ignored altogether. Any additions and/or corrections to the information presented herein will be gratefully acknowledged. Write to: Daniel Roberts, 518 Marshall Dr., West Chester, Penn. 19380.

Acknowledgments

    I would like to acknowledge the help of Bob Gray, who brought my attention to some of these shared covers. Paul Payne was especially helpful in providing information I lacked first-hand regarding the Bantam dust-jacketed covers. Those same cover similarities were also noted by Piet Schreuders on page 85 of his book, PAPERBACKS, U.S.A.: A GRAPHIC HISTORY, 1939-1959. Finally, Kevin Hancer makes note of the Avon 78/105 and Avon 104/Avon Murder Mystery Monthly 13 shared covers on page 48 of his PAPERBACK PRICE GUIDE NO. 2.

Isador N. Steinberg: Profile of an Artist
by Piet Schreuders

"Step up, ladies and gentlemen, and view the ninth Wonder of the Modern World! Artist, painter, writer, wit (of a sort), class cartoonist, Socialist, post-Impressionist, Cubust, Realist, reader of THE MASSES etc. etc. Jack-of-all-trades? Yes, and a master of every one!" Thus wrote the Orange High School Year Book 1917.

The subject, Izzy Steinberg, was then 17 years old--but now, at age 83, most of this description still very much applies. For half a century Mr. Isador N. Steinberg has led a commercial art studio which is still turning out high-quality artwork today. In addition, he spends much time on fine art, painting for gallery shows; he calls fine art his "first and greatest love."

Isador Steinberg made paperback history 44 years ago by painting the first cover for any mass-market paperback: Pocket Book no. 1. When I visited Mr. Steinberg in his spacious studio apartment in New York's upper East side, I asked him how he came to receive this historic assignment.

"I had been doing hardcover jackets for my friend Philip Van Doren Stern at Simon and Schuster since 1936; when Pocket Books started, he introduced me to Robert DeGraff. The first title was LOST HORIZON. I brought a sketch, they liked it, and I redid it larger, in full color. Then I did a second one, and another one, I kept on doing them. I didn't know anyone else who was doing it at that time, I may have been the only one."

Philip Van Doren Stern was Production Manager for Pocket Books, as well as editor and

Piet Schreuders is the author of *Paperbacks, U.S.A.*

Press Proof of the first Pocket Book cover, designed by Steinberg

One of Steinberg's poster designs for the War Department

I.N. Steinberg in 1939
(photo by Philip Van Doren Stern)

A recent portrait

author. He had started out as advertising manager for a radio company in Newark, New Jersey, and it was in that capacity that he met and became friends with Steinberg, in the early 1930s. Later, Stern became a designer and art director in New York. His work for the Simon and Schuster edition of THE BIBLE: DESIGNED TO BE READ AS LIVING LITERATURE (1936) earned him an award in the "50 books of the Year" (a yearly exhibition sponsored by the American Institute of Graphic Arts). It should be noted that the handlettering of the title page of the prize-winning book had actually been done by I. N. Steinberg.

Isador Steinberg is happy to talk about his career. Behind the glasses, his eyes are sparkling with mirth as he recounts his meetings with, it seems, the most famous people and the most important painters and designers of this century. "You know," he says, "before you wrote your first letter, I was thinking: something ought to be done about the history of book jackets. I did those first covers, I ought to get credit for them. I was thinking it on and off through the years, but a little more strongly immediately before your letter came." During the few times I visit him, he shows me his work: the paintings that are lining the walls, drawers and portfolios containing press proofs, originals, and book jackets. There are some sixty book jackets, thirty books with illustrations, as well as several maps, endpaper designs, advertising illustrations and Army posters; and all this must be only the tip of the iceberg, because as usual, most material was never returned by the clients.

From his conversation, which is rich in detail and full of anecdotes, one gets a picture of the artist's early career before Pocket Books. He was born in Odessa, Russia, on June 14, 1900. His father left Russia in 1905, and went to New York by himself; after two years of living in London the family was reunited in New York. They

Four Pocket Book covers painted by Isador Steinberg

moved to New Jersey, to West Orange at first, and then to Orange and East Orange. Izzy attened High School there. At East Orange High School he won a national poster contest as well as a scholarship to the School of Design and Liberal Arts, where he studied for two years under Jonas Lie. Supporting himself by mixing paints in the art department of the Einson-Freeman Lithograph Company, he joined the Art Students League of New York to study under John Sloan, Max Weber and John Bridgman.

When Steinberg and two fellow ASL students, Julian Wehr and Nasif Attayr, decided to go to Maine to paint for six months, he had to quit his job; and, he says, "I never worked for anybody again after that. I freelanced." The cartoonist Art Young (who was a client of a laundry run by Steinberg's aunt) sent him to the office of the Socialist magazine THE MASSES, where artists like Sloan, Weber and Stuart Davis used to work. Here he did his first commercial work. He also produced displays for motion picture houses, showcards for stores (containing cartoons and lettering), etc. While Isador worked, his "sweetheart" Polly used to go around organizing the accounts.

After his marriage to Polly he secured a steady income by supplying all the artwork for a big department store in Newark. They had so much work for him that he had to hire four artists to help him, thus forming the "Steinberg Studios" which, allowing for some name changes, are still functioning today.

In 1935 he moved to New York with his wife and two children, and opened a studio at 68 Washington Square South. Through his friendship with Stern, he received bookjacket assignments from Simon and Schuster, and the art director at Macy's department store, Sanford E. Gerard, provided him with $10,000 worth of work a year.

One account led to another. When Philip Van Doren Stern wrote THE MAN WHO KILLED LINCOLN

Book jacket design for Simon and Schuster. This jacket caught the attention of the Random House art director who subsequently gave many assignments to Steinberg, including the Elliot Paul books.

Pocket Books cover (1939): illustration and lettering.

Book jacket for Tower Books

Book jacket for Random House The lettering was "cannibalized" by Immerman & Hoffman in 1944

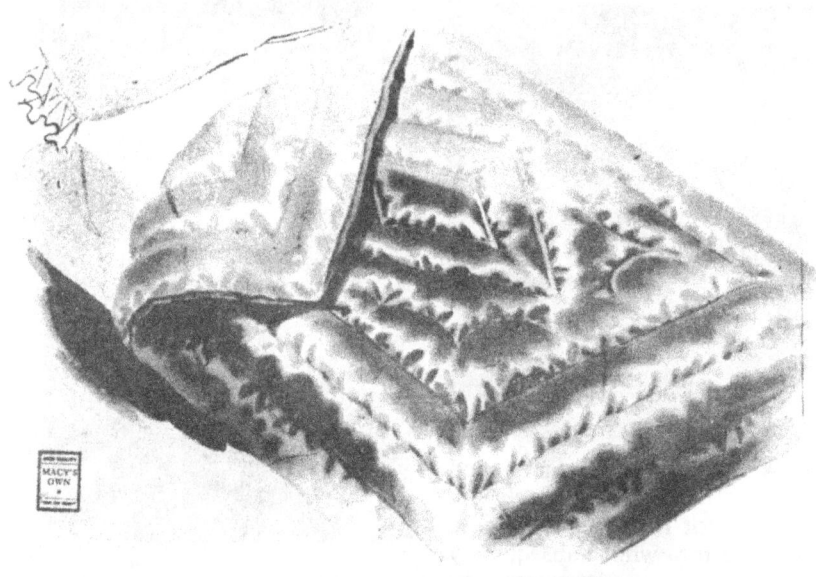

SUPRE-MACY* GOOSEDOWN COMFORTER

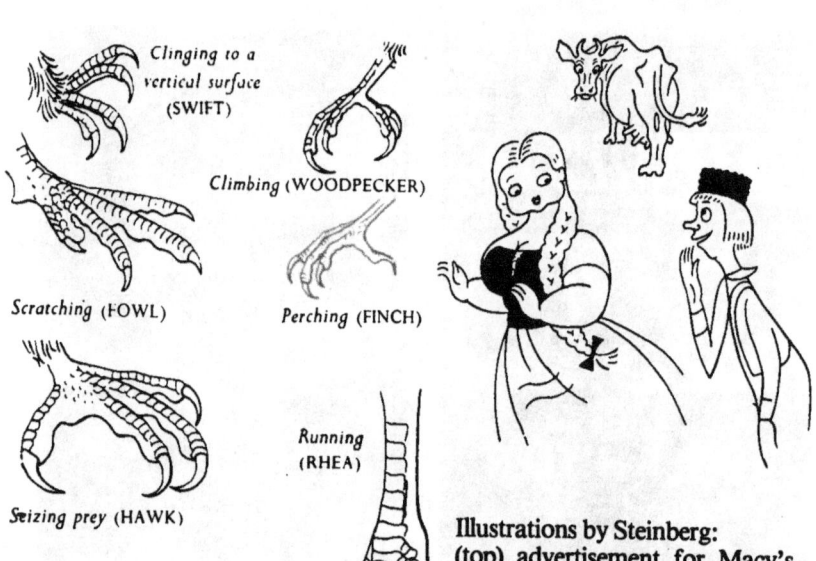

Illustrations by Steinberg: (top) advertisement for Macy's (left) illustration for *Columbia-Viking Desk Encyclopedia*, 1953 (right) illustration for *Mister and Mistress* (Dial Press)

for Random House, Steinberg did the cover; when Sanford Gerard wrote HOW GOOD IS YOUR TASTE? for Doubleday, Steinberg illustrated it. His jacket for ONE AMERICAN AND HIS ATTEMPT AT EDUCATION (Simon and Schuster) caught the attention of the Random House art director, Jacobs, who let him design all book jackets for the Elliot Paul novels, among others. Other publisher clients include Harcourt Brace, Macmillan, World, Viking and Little, Brown.

When the Second World War started, there was an immediate need for graphics: instruction manuals, posters, educational material. Macy's art director, Sanford Gerard, started working as art director for the Pentagon, together with Fred Brauer, and they both recommended Steinberg. Steinberg received a three-month contract as an Expert Consultant to the Secretary of War in Washington and was in charge of drawings for the "Books for the Army" department. After these three months, he returned to New York, but continued working for the Army with his studio, which by now was called "Production & Illustration Company." Working at the studio at the time were Michael Geiger, Herman Temple, Philip Fox, Sidney Gold, Paul Jenisch, Mannis Wesson, Laverne Evans, Hal Stone and Harry Lapeau; William Golden, who later became famous as the art director for CBS, worked for the studio as layout man for a while.

Three studios in New York produced artwork for the Army: the famous Charles E. Cooper Studios, who had the best realistic illustrators; the Lawrence Studios; and Steinberg's studio, which began to specialize in technical illustration. "Because I was willing to study, "Mr. Steinberg says, "I found I was able to do many drawings that others started but couldn't finish. I had done illustrations for a book called THE EVOLUTION OF PHYSICS by Albert Einstein and Leopold Infeld (Simon and Schuster, 1938) and discovered I could do diagrams, technical illustrations as well as educational cartoons quite easily." Between 1944 and 1946, his studio produced literally thousands of drawings of complicated war machinery and illustrations for training manuals. For a field manual on Physical Training, the studio churned out 1900 drawings of the human figure, for which the man in charge of the said manual, major Paige, posed on the Steinberg studio floor. Says Steinberg: "For a manual on Military Roentgenology, we got Lavern, our only female artist, to draw the parts of the male anatomy. But we couldn't get her to react!"

Of his wartime work, Mr. Steinberg now says, "It was not only much more profitable, but also more urgent; I felt patriotic. The reason my studio progressed was that a lot of the artists wanted to work for me because I was doing war work, which would excuse them from the Army. And I was proud of meeting all these people at the Pentagon; I thought my work was very worthwhile, I thought I was fighting Hitler!"

After the war, Steinberg continued to specialize in technical illustration. For THE COLUMBIA-VIKING DESK ENCYCLOPEDIA (Viking Press, 1953) he produced twenty plates containing over 100 illustrations. He actually enjoyed this work, he says, while showing me a plate of different shapes of bird feet: "I learned a lot while drawing these." He made 700 drawings for THE DICTIONARY OF ANTIQUES AND THE DECORATIVE ARTS (Scribner's Sons, 1957); he illustrated the PRICE GUIDE TO AMERICAN CUT GLASS (M. Barrows & Co., 1967).

"I didn't realize the variety of the work I did," Steinberg now says, "it happened too fast! But I think variety is important. You have to keep learning new things, in order to keep alive. Every time I get a stupid layout and I have to correct it in order to do the work,

I have to think, be an art director myself."
Isador Steinberg has certainly succeeded in
"keeping alive" in this way. Over dinner at
a restaurant, he puts a mathematical riddle to
me by drawing a diagram on a paper napkin. Ten
months later, I still have not found an answer.

"It is a dubious question," the artist
reflects, "whether I should have braved the
hardship and stuck to painting, but I found
commercial art so easy! Seeing now the volume
of the work I did, I can't help thinking: If
I'd spent all that energy in painting--"

His wife cuts in: "I resent you saying
that. I think you've done very well."

Steinberg chuckles, and says: "Anyway, my
commercial career enabled me to put two boys
through college. I always say: Money does not
bring happiness--but it keeps you in contact with
your children!"

Design by Steinberg

Science-Fiction and Fantasy in the Dell Mapbacks
by W. H. Lyles

Dell "mapbacks" (1942-1951) featured a great deal of genre fiction, mostly mysteries, westerns, and romances. Little science-fiction or fantasy appeared, however, due to the prejudice of Lloyd Smith, the early editor-in-chief of the Dell books. Smith worked for Western Printing & Lithographing (Racine, Wisconsin), which produced and designed the paperbacks; he disliked science-fiction and felt it would not sell. But Don Ward, another Western employee and the resident expert on westerns, introduced a few science-fiction titles, though none used that term on cover blurbs.[1]

Two Dell books by the respectable H. G. Wells were mapbacks: THE FIRST MEN IN THE MOON (#201, 1947) and THE INVISIBLE MAN (#269, 1948). The first is an attractive book, the first paperback appearance of that title. Earl Sherwan's front cover, while suggesting the nature of the lunar surface, does not depict any specific scene in the novel. Few Dell covers of the 1940's did: they used a "design" approach, like a poster, the idea of Western's art director, William Strohmer, and his assistant, George A. Frederiksen. The back cover of THE FIRST MEN IN THE MOON--executed by Ruth Belew--is unique among the Dell maps: the only one of a planet or satellite (except Earth). Nicely drawn, it is also totally useless; Wells mentions no topographical detail. In his satire on human events, Wells even goes out of his way to ignore topography.

THE INVISIBLE MAN, a more biting satire than THE FIRST MEN, features on the Dell edition an airbrushed cover by Gerald Gregg, who painted most of the Dell covers of the 1940's. The

Invasion from Mars (Dell #305)

cover cleverly captures the title character's essential vagueness and lack of detail. The back-cover map is of limited usefulness; both the village of Iping (in West Sussex, England) and Sussex are only vaguely described by the author. A map of London--scene of the Invisible Man's narrative, Chapters 19-23--would be more appropriate and welcome.

The only other science-fiction mapback is an anthology, INVASION FROM MARS (#305, 1949) credited as being "selected" by Orson Welles. The real compiler was Don Ward, who put together most of the Dell anthologies, including the Hitchcock ones. Ward remembers that Welles changed one sentence in the preface; Ward did the rest. The anthology contains nine stories, ranging from the radio script of Welles' adaptation of H. G. Wells' THE WAR OF THE WORLDS to Theodore Sturgeon's sprawling description of a post-Holocaust earth in "Farewell to Eden." Only three of the stories concern Mars. The cover--the only Dell cover by Malcolm Smith-- is not too distinguished, but it does make the book seem clearly science-fiction. The map illustrates Ray Bradbury's "The Million Year Picnic." Unnecessary, but clever and colorful, the map contains in its cryptic banner, "Martians Seen Here," a key to the story's end. Bradbury wasn't too excited by the map; "it doesn't depict my dream of Mars at all," he responded to my query.

Dell introduced more science-fiction in the late 1950's, but the company never seemed too comfortable with the genre, nor even with fantasy. The Dell fantasy titles included two books by Edgar Rice Burroughs, two adaptations of books by H. Rider Haggard, and three others. Dell also published two "horror" titles.

One of Edgar Rice Burroughs' non-series titles was CAVE GIRL (#320, 1949). It is not Burroughs at his best: a typical adventure where

Front cover of H. Rider Haggard's *King Solomon's Mines* (at right) and Dell Mapback (below)

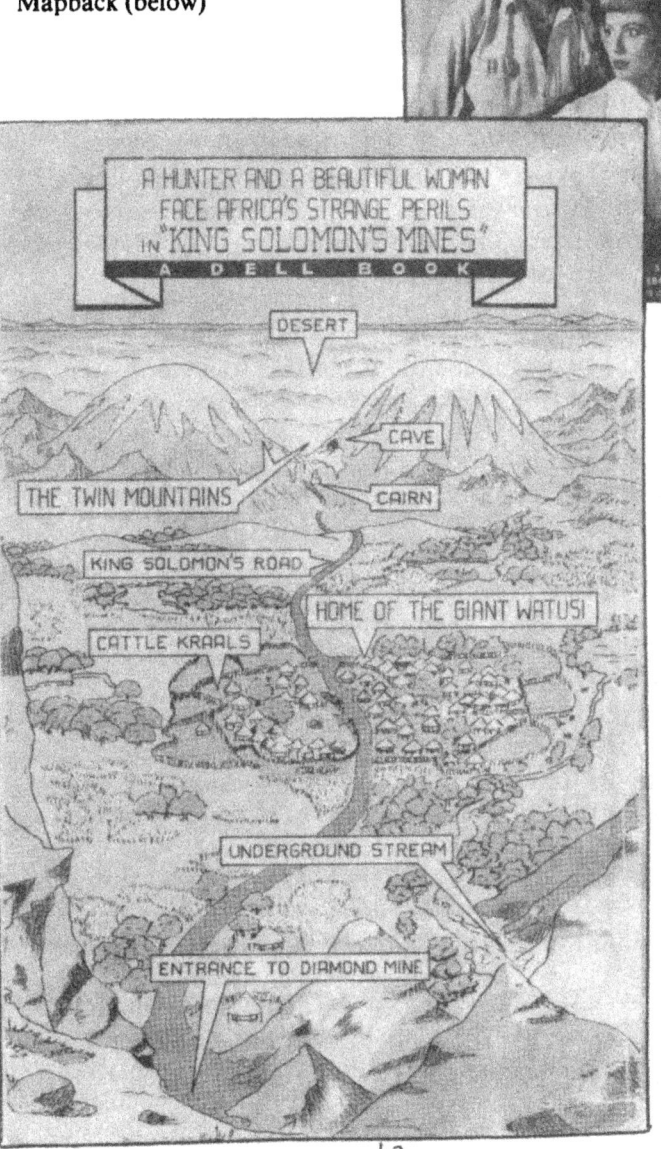

a sissified dandy becomes savagely respectable. Jean des Vignes' front cover shows the titillating title character, Nadara, dancing (See pages 146-147). The back cover elaborates the isolated stone-age island where the book occurs; it includes 14 key locales, including "Thandar Fights Flatfoot" and "Nadara Loses Trail." A reader would be hard pressed to follow the map while reading the book; only Burroughs would be able to make concrete his sketchy verbal descriptions.[2]

TARZAN AND THE LOST EMPIRE (#536, 1951), Burroughs' other Dell paperback, is a credible inclusion in the Tarzan series. Its cover seems to represent Johnny Weismuller; most of Robert Stanley's covers were patterned after Stanley or his wife, Rhoda. The book's character list is inclusive, but it lacks Tarzan's great apes; few Dell lists included animals. The map is accurate and detailed, at least in relationship to the overwhelming amount of detail provided by Burroughs.[3]

Two Dell books appeared under the byline of H. Rider Haggard. SHE (#339, 1949) is "retold" by Don Ward; KING SOLOMON'S MINES (#433, 1950) is "fictionized" from the 1950 film version by Jean Francis Webb. For SHE, Ward omitted Haggard's opening frame, the footnotes, and most of the novel's peripheral information. The Dell edition's front cover (signed as by "Maurieri"?), is superb, picturing Ayesha ("She Who Must Be Obeyed") in the life-renewing flames. The character list is excellent. And the map presents an accurate, colorful rendering of the city of Kôr, in east central Africa, in the 1800's. The map is based on Haggard's own, which appears in most editions of the original novel.

For the Dell edition of KING SOLOMON'S MINES, Jean Francis Webb performed more drastic surgery than had Don Ward. But Webb was working with a movie script as well as Haggard's novel. Webb did other such projects; he remembers that he usually had 2-3 weeks to do the novelization. Sometimes he was allowed to see a preliminary screening of the film; more often he was just supplied with a script. His version of MINES changes Haggard's version drastically; for example, the climactic battle between tribes in Haggard's book is here changed to a ritualistic battle between two tribal chiefs. Perhaps the filmmakers felt that was cheaper. And the Dell/film edition adds a woman to the book--the oddest change of all, since Haggard goes out of his way to avoid female characters in the novel.

The front cover of the Dell edition of KING SOLOMON'S MINES is from the 1950 film, far inferior to the 1937 version with Paul Robeson and Cedric Hardwicke. The character list omits Bizu (the Zabamari chief), Gagool (the evil Watusi), and Lulu the monkey. The map is well done and generally accurate, even if the artist seemed at pains to make the twin mountains more breastlike than necessary. Haggard's own map of the region is not included. It should be, or at least incorporated into the Dell map. The Dell edition calls the area Watusiland (1897-1898); Haggard termed it Kukuanaland (1880's).

Philip Wylie's THE SAVAGE GENTLEMAN (#85, 1945), a borderline fantasy, is often referred to by critics as a precursor of Superman. The novel seems to have more similarities to the Tarzan books, however: its sill, superficial philosophies, including the old paradox about the necessity of savagery in civilization; its cardboard characters, and its quick pace. Even a reader prepared to dislike Wylie might find himself seduced by the easiness of the prose. The cover, representative of the oxymoronic title, is by Gerald Gregg; it is not one of his best. But the cluttered map is beautiful: its excellent detail, appropriate color, and accuracy present an inviting view for an undecided reader. An exacting reader could argue that the savannah between the pasture and the moutain should be included (see p. 44), but the map captures most of the rest of Wylie's described places. Unlike many Dell maps, this one is not at all to scale; it features instead cartouches and symbolic designs.

Avon also published an edition of THE SAVAGE GENTLEMAN (#390, 1952). Like the Dell edition, this also has a character list, but it tells too much of the plot. The front cover is typical of Avon's lurid covers of the 1950's. The back-cover is a dull blurb.

Frederic Arnold Kummer's LADIES IN HADES (#415, 1950) presents one of the more colorful and amusing maps in the Dell series. We see an aerial view of a small section of Hell (with an inset of Hell's "Civic Center"). Most of this Virgilian guide is the artist's own effort. The author mentions that Eve's home is in Figleaf Park, near the Bottomless Pit, and that Salome's villa is the suburban Jezebel Farms, far from the Pit, but the placement of Charon's Ferry, Lucrezia Borgia's house, the Gehenna Gazette, the Cloven Hoff Inn, and other colorfully-named attractions is entirely the artist's contribution. In fact, not all of these places are even mentioned by Kummer: no Pluto Pictures for instance, although (one page 37) Satan mentions a picture studio named Famous Sinners, Inc. Despite the inaccuracies, the additions, and the mild pastels (the map has no deep reds!), this is an entertaining graphic complement to a mildly amusing book.

Another Dell fantasy, similar only in that its purpose is to amuse, is David Stern's FRANCIS (#507, 1951), a collection of several "Francis the Talking Mule" stories. The book has a decorated back cover with a small map and six other insets, all arranged as a "chart."

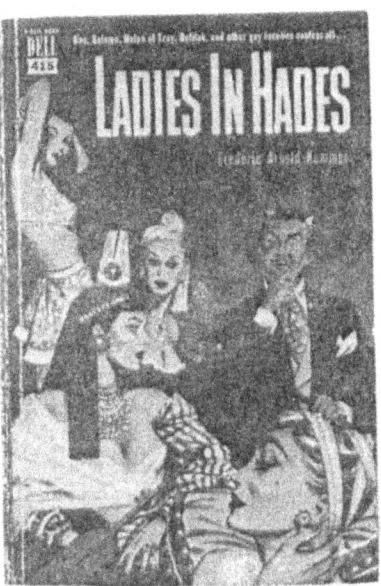

Front cover of *Tarzan and the Lost Empire* (above) and mapback (below)

Front cover of *Ladies in Hades* (above) and Mapback (at right)

Tarzan of the Apes and a young scientist face death on the sands of the arena in a lost Roman province in the heart of Africa.

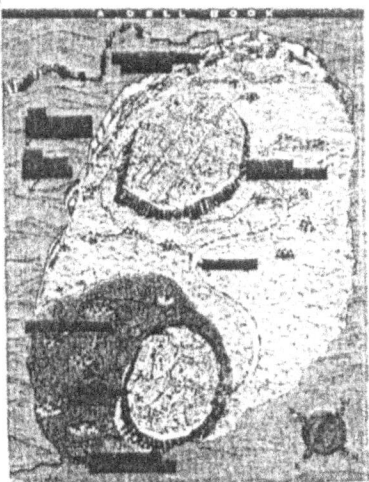

H.G. Well's *The First Men in the Moon* (Dell #201)

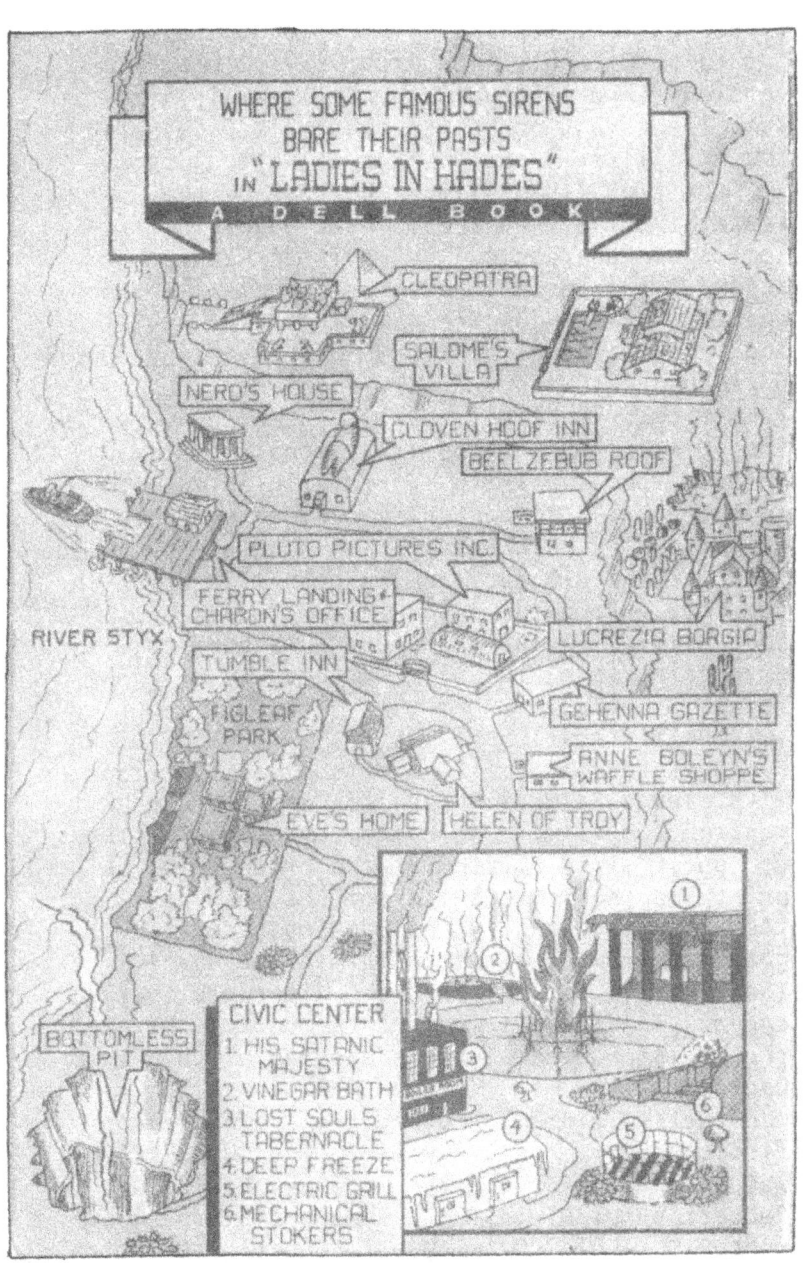

No detailed map is possible, since Stern describes no locality in any detail. Incidentally, for those who only know Francis from his film versions (Francis' voice by Chill Wills, the dumb lieutenant portrayed by Donald O'Connor), the novelistic Francis flies as well as talks.

Dell published little horror--neither Western nor Dell wanted to make waves in its comics or paperbacks. But editors managed to sneak in two borderline horror novels: Gaston Leroux' THE PHANTOM OF THE OPERA (#24, 1943) and Irina Karlova's DREADFUL HOLLOW (#125, 1946). DREADFUL HOLLOW is a dreary novel of vague vampirism. The front cover, by George A. Frederiksen, was deliberately done to imitate Gerald Gregg's paintings; Frederiksen rubbed in the pastels to approximate Gregg's airbrushed effects. The back cover is an accurate overhead view of "The Grange," central vampiric scene in the book. Readers may be interested to know that William Faulkner adapted this book to screenplay form; the film was not, to my knowledge, produced.

Dell's edition of THE PHANTOM OF THE OPERA appeared in the same year as the film version with Claude Rains. But Dell's edition does not mention the film. The cover, by Gregg, pictures a vaguely silly Phantom at the organ. The "blueprint" map seems accurate for the most part, but the artist apparently included much detail gathered from sources other than the novel. (Some detail derives from the afterword that appears in many editions of the book.) Perhaps the artist had access to a diagram of the Paris Opéra.

Dell did plan other editions of science-fiction and fantasy. Cyril Judd's GUNNER CADE was scheduled for the 25¢ in 1952, Lewis Padgett's MUTANT in 1953, Theodore Sturgeon's E PLURIBUS UNICORN in 1954, and George O. Smith's HELLFLOWER in 1954. Guy Endore's THE WEREWOLF OF PARIS was scheduled as #D376 in 1956. But a

Dell vice-president objected to the anti-Catholic elements in the novel, as former Dell editor Allan Barnard remembers. More such fiction occurred in the Dell First Edition line, although even there it was often disguised. Even Jack Finney's THE BODY SNATCHERS (First Edition #42, 1955), to judge from the cover, seems more a suspense novel than science-fiction. (Finney's working title, by the way, was "A Fall of Small Frogs." A good change.) The cover of Kendall Foster Crossen's YEAR OF CONSENT (First Edition #32, 1954) hardly suggests any strong futuristic elements. Not until the 1960's, when Kurt Vonnegut made science-fiction respectable, did Dell seem comfortable with the genre. (Dell later signed a million-dollar deal with Vonnegut; by that time Vonnegut had become a mainstream writer.) Even today, Dell publishes little science-fiction and fantasy in comparison with Ace, Ballantine, or Bantam.

Notes

1. The Dell editions of the Alfred Hitchcock anthologies are not discussed here. See Billy C. Lee and Charlotte Laughlin, "Alfred Hitchcock: Dell Paperbacks," PAPERBACK QUARTERLY, Vol 3 no. 1 (Spring 1980), pp 23-36.
2. THE CAVE GIRL map also appears in J. B. Post, AN ATLAS OF FANTASY (Baltimore: The Mirage Press, 1973), p. 189; second edition (N.Y.: Ballantine, 1979), p. 77.
3. Burroughs' own map of the area is reproduced in Post's ATLAS, p. 175; second edition, p. 65. Another version appears in Alberto Manguel and Gianni Guadalupi, THE DICTIONARY OF IMAGINARY PLACES (N.Y.: Macmillan, 1980), p. 71.

Nelson Algren in Paperback: A Checklist
by Paul Garon

What follows is a checklist of the appearances of Nelson Algren's works in paperback. Foreign editions have been omitted. Nearly all the books referred to have been examined by me, often in multiple copies, and when a book was not available for examination, "not seen" is noted in the appropriate place. It is hoped that the publication of such a checklist will create an opportunity to examine the books listed as "not seen," and I further hope that owners of these books will contact me, so that additions, corrections, and fill-ins of miscellaneous data can be published.

Following standard terminology, an "edition" or "new edition" refers to a separate or new setting of the type. A "printing" or "impression" (within an edition) refers to a separate trip to press. As we know, with early paperbacks many printings may be concealed; a book may be reprinted five or ten times with the same cover and issue number, and it's often impossible to know how many times such a book was reprinted. As an example, if Avon had not supplied the printing history of NEVER COME MORNING on the copyright page of Avon 419, we would never have known that it was at least a 5th printing. With companies like Pocket Books, we are given a complete (hopefully accurate) printing history on the copyright page, and while most companies did not follow that practice (Avon did it only occasionally), there are often other clues like the state of the advertisements, cover price, etc. I have used such clues whenever possible. I have also drawn some inspiration and/or assistance from earlier Algren checklists by Kenneth G. McCollum and Richard Studing and from Reginald and Burgess' CUMULATIVE PAPERBACK INDEX.

Never Come Morning by Nelson Algren (Avon T-108)

SOMEBODY IN BOOTS

Nelson Algren's first book was SOMEBODY IN BOOTS, published by Vanguard in 1935. According to Harvey Swados (ed. THE AMERICAN WRITER AND THE GREAT DEPRESSION. Indianapolis: Bobbs-Merrill, 1966) only 770 copies were printed. It was first published by Avon in an abridged edition retitled THE JUNGLE (1957), but not until well after their great success with two later works, NEVER COME MORNING (1948) and THE NEON WILDERNESS (1949). The Avon printings of THE JUNGLE were issued with two different issue numbers and two different covers. Both T-185 and T-324 were abridged, Berkley S1125 (1965) being the first unabridged paperback of SOMEBODY IN BOOTS. The dedication that appeared in the original Vanguard edition was dropped by Avon, but it reappeared in the Berkley edition: "Dedicated to those innumerable Thousands: The Homeless Boys of America."

NEVER COME MORNING

A more complicated and exciting history is shown by Algren's second book, NEVER COME MORNING, which had at least two printings in its original Harper edition; the first printing was in 1942. Avon issued the book with four different numbers and essentially two different covers, yet there were at least seven Avon printings. On the copyright page of T-108 Avon complicated matters by calling it the "seventh Avon Edition" (actually the 6th printing); yet if the print figures they gave (in 419) were correct, there probably were "one million copies now in print," as they indicated in T-108. Algren had won the first National Book Award for fiction in 1950 for THE MAN WITH THE GOLDEN ARM, and the cover of T-108 informs us of this fact. All Avon editions of NEVER COME MORNING

were "specially revised," i.e. abridged. In
1963 and 1965 Harper issued NEVER COME MORNING
as a trade paperback, first as a Colophon edition
and then as a rack size Perennial edition. These
editions were unabridged, as was the subsequent
1968 edition published by Berkley. The Harper
Colophon edition has a new dedication, to Candida
Donadio, his literary agent, and a new preface
by Algren. All subsequent editions and printings
are unabridged, contain the new preface and have
the new dedication. The original dedication,
"For Bernice," appeared only in the original
Harper edition of 1942.

THE NEON WILDERNESS

The cover of Avon 222 (1949), THE NEON
WILDERNESS, was the same cover that adorned the
comic, INTIMATE CONFESSIONS #1, and for this
reason it has become, perhaps, the Algren book
most familiar to paperback collectors. (It was
originally published by Doubleday in 1947.)
Avon reprinted the book in 1952 as Avon 424 with
a similar cover, changed only to the extent of
the rear wrap and a short blurb added to the
front wrap; they printed it again in 1956 (T-125)
with an entirely different cover. In 1960
Hill and Wang published the book in a trade
size paperback, and they reprinted it two years
later. A new introduction by Algren appeared
first in the Hill and Wang edition as well as
in the Berkley edition of 1965 (S1103) and in
later Hill and Wang printings. Avon 222 and
424 both contain the original dedication to
Algren's parents; Avon T-125 contains no dedication. Beginning with the Hill and Wang edition
and in all subsequent paperback editions and
printings, the dedication becomes, "For Ruth
Reinhardt of Jazz Ltd., Chicago."

THE MAN WITH THE GOLDEN ARM

The Neon Wilderness by Nelson Algren (Avon #222)

Pocket Books published THE MAN WITH THE GOLDEN ARM in 1951 (#757); Doubleday had published it in 1949, and it had won the National Book Award for fiction in 1950. According to Reginald and Burgess (CUMULATIVE PAPERBACK INDEX 1939-1959. Detroit: Gale, 1973), 1953 was the date it was published as a Cardinal edition (C-31), but I've never been able to locate a "First Cardinal Printing." The second Cardinal printing was done with a movie tie-in cover in January, 1956 and reached at least a "7th Cardinal Printing" in June, 1956. While I've not seen an example of the 4th and 6th Cardinal printing, it is likely that the 2nd-7th all used the same movie tie-in art work.

As we know, dust jackets were often used on paperbacks to give new life (and art work) to old covers. Pocket Book #757 was issued in a dust jacket and the dust jacket was designated "C-31." The art work on the dust jacket is certainly more interesting than the art work found inside on PB #757, and it seems likely that the dust jacket alone was actually the "First Cardinal Printing." Further, in the printing history given on the copyright page of the second Cardinal printing, 1951 is given as the year of publication of the Cardinal edition, a date at variance with the year given by Reginald and Burgess. In any case, no actual Cardinal edition was published until 1956, the year of the "2nd Cardinal printing. 1951 (or 1953) was the year of publication of the Cardinal C-31 dust jacket alone!

In 1964 Fawcett/Crest published THE MAN WITH THE GOLDEN ARM (t725), and it was reprinted at least three times, each time with a new cover. In 1977 Penguin published a rack size trade paper edition that is still in print. THE MAN WITH THE GOLDEN ARM had at least eight different covers in its paperback editions, more than any other Algren title. The original dedication,

"To the Newberry Library of Chicago...." disappeared in the Fawcett/Crest edition and reappeared in the Penguin edition.

CHICAGO: CITY ON THE MAKE

CHICAGO: CITY ON THE MAKE was originally published in 1951 by Doubleday and was never published in a mass market paperback. It did have two later incarnations as a quality size paperback, both published by Angel Island Publications. Each Angel Island edition was enlarged considerably, first with a lengthy new introduction by Algren (published as a Contact Edition in 1961) and then with a lengthy epilogue by Algren (published as an Angel Island publication, n.d.). The epilogue was titled "Ode to Lowerfinksville" and appears so in all but 100 copies. In these 100 copies, specially printed for Algren at his insistence, the epilogue title is "Ode to Kissassville or: Gone on the Arfy-Darfy." The original dedication was to Carl Sandburg, the second edition was dedicated to Herman and Marilou Kogan and the third edition was dedicated to Joan Baez.

A WALK ON THE WILD SIDE

A WALK ON THE WILD SIDE was algren's own favorite of his novels; it was published by Farrar, Straus and Cudahy in 1956, and it was first published in paperback by Fawcett/Crest in 1957 (d157). It went through at least nine Crest printings with a least five different covers. Most interesting is the fact that the cover for the 3rd Crest printing, which was abandoned for the movie tie-in cover used on the 4th, 5th and 6th Crest printings, was brought back into use for the 7th Crest printing when the movie tie-in cover had outlived its usefulness. It is also worth noting that the

Arthur Shay photograph of Algren, used as the art work on the original Farrar dust jacket, was also used on the front cover (as art work) or back cover of all Crest printings except those using movie tie-in art work. In 1977 a rack size trade paperback was published by Penguin.

NELSON ALGREN'S OWN BOOK OF LONESOME MONSTERS

NELSON ALGREN'S BOOK OF LONESOME MONSTERS was Algren's only "paperback original," its publication by Lancer in 1962 (73-409) preceding its cloth publication (by Bernard Geis Associates) by one year. Algren edited this collection of thirteen stories, and he included one story of his own and added his own preface. Lancer reprinted the collection with a new cover as #33016, n.d. The cloth edition contained two additional stories and notes on the contributors, but no new material by Algren was added.

WHO LOST AN AMERICAN?

The printing history of WHO LOST AN AMERICAN? is unusual. It was originally published by Andre Deutsch in England in 1963, and was published by Macmillan in this country later the same year. Although it has appeared in paperback in England, it has never been published as a paperback in this country; it is the only one of Algren's books about which that can be said.

CONVERSATIONS WITH NELSON ALGREN

H. E. F. Donahue's CONVERSATIONS WITH NELSON ALGREN was published in paperback by Berkley in 1965 (S1134), within months of the publication of the Berkley editions of SOMEBODY IN BOOTS and THE NEON WILDERNESS. Hill and Wang had published the cloth edition a year earlier. Neither edition was reprinted.

THE LAST CAROUSEL

Algren's final book, THE LAST CAROUSEL, was published in 1973, again by Putnam. Warner Paperback Library published the paper edition in 1975 (79-727), and it was not reprinted.

SOMEBODY IN BOOTS

PUBLISHER/BOOK NO./YEAR	PRICE	COVER TYPE	REMARKS
Avon T-185 1957 (THE JUNGLE)	35¢	SIB 1	Abridged
Avon T-324 1959 (THE JUNGLE)	35¢	SIB 2	Abridged
Berkley S1125	75¢	SIB 3	Unabridged, 1st appearance of new preface

NEVER COME MORNING

PUBLISHER/BOOK NO./YEAR	PRICE	COVER TYPE	REMARKS
Avon 185 1948	25¢	NCM 1a	Specially revised(abridged)
Avon 419 1952	25¢	NCM 1b	Specially revised(abridged), rear wrap changed. Copyright page contains printing history: Nov 1948 200,000 Feb 1949 200,000 Apr 1949 200,000 Jan 1950 150,000 Dec 1951 200,000 950,000
Avon T-108 1955	35¢	NCM 2	On copyright page, "seventh Avon Edition" and "one million copies now in print."
Avon T223 1958	35¢	NCM 2	Same as above, but without "seventh Avon Edition."
Harper Colophon 15 1963	$1.75	NCM 3	Unabridged; 1st appearance of new preface; new dedication.
Harper Perennial P4406 1965	60¢	NCM 4	Same as above
Berkley N1583 1968	95¢	NCM 5	Same as above

THE NEON WILDERNESS

PUBLISHER/BOOK NO./YEAR	PRICE	COVER TYPE	REMARKS
Avon 222 1949	25¢	NW 1a	
Avon 424 1952	25¢	NW 1b	Review blurb added to front wrap, rear wrap changed.
Avon T-125 1956	35¢	NW 2	
Hill & Wang 1960			not seen
Hill & Wang AC27 1962	$1.45	NW 3	First appearance of new introduction and new dedication (probably also appear in 1st Hill and Wang printing 1960, above).
Berkley S1103 1965	75¢	NW 4	(same as above)
Hill & Wang			Not seen
Hill & Wang 0027 1975	$4.95	NW 5	(same as 2nd H & W printing, 1962, above)

THE MAN WITH THE GOLDEN ARM

PUBLISHER/BOOK NO./YEAR	PRICE	COVER TYPE	REMARKS
Pocket Book 757 1951	25¢	MWGA 1	
Cardinal C-31 1951?	35¢	MWGA 2	"1st Cardinal Printing," exists only as dj on PB 757?
Cardinal C-31 Jan-1956	35¢	MWGA 3	"2nd Cardinal Printing"
Cardinal C-31 Jan-1956	35¢	MWGA 3	"3rd Cardinal Printing"
Cardinal C-31 1956	35¢	MWGA 3	Not seen
Cardinal C-31 Feb-1956	35¢	MWGA 3	"5th Cardinal Printing"
Cardinal C-31 1956	35¢	MWGA 3	Not seen
Cardinal C-31 Jun-1956	35¢	MWGA 3	"7th Cardinal Printing"
Fawcett/Crest T725 Jun-1964	75¢	MWGA 4	Dedication disappears
Fawcett/Prem. M511 Nov-1970	95¢	MWGA 5	
Fawcett/Crest M956 n.d.	95¢	MWGA 6	
Fawcett/Crest M1184 n.d.	95¢	MWGA 7	
Penguin 1977	$2.50	MWGA 8	Dedication reappears

CHICAGO: CITY ON THE MAKE

PUBLISHER/BOOK NO./YEAR	PRICE	COVER TYPE	REMARKS
Angel Island 1961	95¢	CCOM 1	A "Contact Edition," trade size; actually the 2nd ed., enlarged.
Angel Island n.d.	$2.45	CCOM 2	The 2nd Angel Island ed., actually the 3rd ed., again enlarged + photographs by S. Deutch. Dedication changes.

A WALK ON THE WILD SIDE

PUBLISHER/BOOK NO./YEAR	PRICE	COVER TYPE	REMARKS
Fawcett/Crest d157 Jan-1957	50¢	WWS 1	
Fawcett/Crest d157 May-1957	50¢	WWS 1	
Fawcett/Crest d377 May-1960	50¢	WWS 2	
Fawcett/Crest d496 Jan-1962	50¢	WWS 3	4th Crest Printing, movie tie-in art work
Fawcett/Crest d496 Apr-1962	50¢	WWS 3	5th Crest Printing, same as above
Fawcett/Crest d496 Sep-1962	?	WWS 3	6th Crest Printing, same as above
Fawcett/Crest d496 Mar-1963	?	WWS 2	7th Crest Printing
Fawcett/Crest t890 n.d.	75¢	WWS 4	?
Fawcett/Crest m1238 n.d.	95¢	WWS 5	?
Penguin 1977	$2.50	WWS 6	

NELSON ALGREN'S OWN BOOK OF LONESOME MONSTERS

PUBLISHER/BOOK NO./YEAR	PRICE	COVER TYPE	REMARKS
Lancer 73-409 1962	60¢	LM 1	The true 1st edition
Lancer 33016 n.d.	$1.25	LM 2	

CONVERSATIONS WITH NELSON ALGREN

PUBLISHER/BOOK NO./YEAR	PRICE	COVER TYPE	REMARKS
Berkley S1134 Sep-1965	75¢	CWNA 1	1st and only paperback printing

NOTES FROM A SEA DIARY

PUBLISHER/BOOK NO./YEAR	PRICE	COVER TYPE	REMARKS
Fawcett/Crest R973 Oct-1966	60¢	NSD 1	1st and only paperback printing

THE LAST CAROUSEL

PUBLISHER/BOOK NO./YEAR	PRICE	COVER TYPE	REMARKS
Warner Paperback Library 79-727 Feb-1975	$1.95	LC 1	1st and only paperback printing

Seeing Double

Popular Library #221 (1949)
cover art by Earle K. Bergey

Un Mystere #87 (1952)

Dutch collector Anton Hermus sent in this staggering example of paperback cover plagiarism.

Covers That Never Were
by Piet Schreuders

The following are two covers by Robert Jonas for Penguin #627: LIGHTHOUSE by Archie Binns, and Bantam #35: A FAREWELL TO ARMS by Ernest Hemingway. Before you run to your paperback shelves to check the numbers on these two extremely rare paperbacks, you might as well know the truth: the books do not exist. These reproductions were made from press-proofs that are in Robert Jonas' possession. They are finished covers, but the books themselves never appeared in this form. Penguin #627 was TOBACCO ROAD (also, incidentally, with a Jonas cover); Bantam #35 was MY DEAR BELLA (with a cover by Thomas Ruzicka and Sydney Hoff). Interestingly, Robert Jonas, after making some minor changes with his unused "Farewell" cover, used the design on THE WORLD OF HISTORY (Mentor M109, 1954).

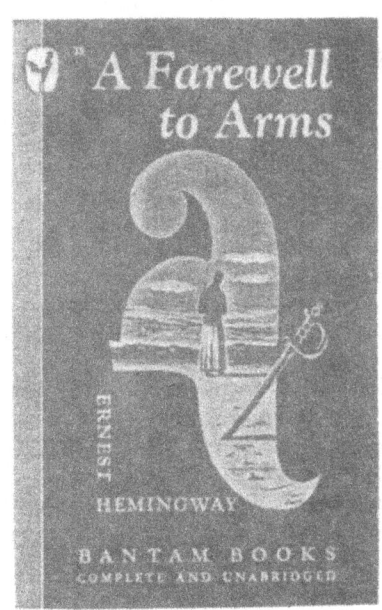

I HAVE THE BEST
I BUY THE BEST

BILL LIPPINCOTT   Paper/Books

I specialize in paperbacks of the 1939-59 period, especially Ace, Avon, Dell, and Popular Library. I have a vast selection of other publishing houses, and a multitude of detective and spicy digests —

Send $1.00 for my current list.

WANTED: in very good or better condition: early paperbacks by Robert Bloch, Frederic Brown, Raymond Chandler, Harlan Ellison, Dashiell Hammett, HPLovecraft, Sax Rohmer, Cornell Woolrich (William Irish). Also Avon, Bart House, Dell 10¢, Crossword Puzzle books, Bergey or Belarski covers (Pop.Lib.), digests, drug oriented paperbacks. And all paperbacks in color section of Paperback Price Guide.

SPECIAL WANTS: Ace D-13, D-15, Avon 285, 298, 314, any L.A.Bantams, and the Diversey digest edition of REFORM SCHOOL GIRL.

I buy and sell the finest in early paperbacks, whether it be the 1st Edition of an important author, a stunning example of vintage cover art, or an obscure publisher's most bizarre title. — I HAVE THE BEST & I BUY THE BEST!

Bill Lippincott —   Paper/Books
Box 506, Bingham, Maine 04920
(207) 672-4888 or 566-7972

www.ingramcontent.com/pod-product-compliance
Lightning Source LLC
Chambersburg PA
CBHW031424040426
42444CB00006B/694